MAXIMUM IMPACT

Writing Short

Say More With Less

Condense the Essence - Leave 'em Satisfied

Maureen F. Sevilla

COPYRIGHT

DEDICATION

This book is dedicated to all authors who share their time and expertise with countless aspiring writers. The real answers to the questions about how to get published, how to write romance, and how to promote a book have always come to me from fellow authors. The research I did on my own over the years would have meant nothing without the generous support of my colleagues. Classes and workshops and explanations, critiques and beta reading from fellow authors who have always been there for each other has meant everything to me. Thank you.

CONTENTS

FOREWORD

For many years, I've been an avid romance reader, writer, and an editor. More recently, I've also been working as a writing coach and an independent editor, expanding my experience beyond content, copy, and romance editing to other genres. I maintain an eclectic taste in reading, which is what keeps me from focusing on one genre when I write.

After being invited to do a presentation about "writing short" for a conference, several notions came to mind. Before I retired from the corporate world to write fiction and edit, I used to write ads, newsletters, catalogues, educational material, and presentations for a marketing company. I clearly understand the reason why writing short needs to provide maximum impact whether writing ad campaigns or taglines or book blurbs. Every word counts.

A few ideas, some painful analysis, and a great deal of research later, I hope to help other authors understand the idea of condensing a concept without losing the essence of the writing. Keep the flavor and the spice even when you choose to reduce the size of the recipe.

The one exceptional thing I identified while preparing the presentation was how to take theme and compress the ideas to efficiently write something short yet interesting. The following are *suggestions*, so as writers, we can... *Condense the essence and leave the reader satisfied.* The magic word is...suggestion.

Editor, Maureen F. Sevilla (aka Author, Eliza March)

1 Chapter - Define Short

We write for a variety of purposes, and some of those purposes we don't even think about. We don't count much of it as writing—yet we need a certain structure and talent to do it well. Short writing includes magazine articles, newspaper articles, obituaries, engagement or marriage announcements, classified ads, advertising in general. For our purpose in this guide, we will concentrate on fiction writing and what tools a writer uses while writing fiction in general and how to apply those tools to shorter goals.

What defines writing short?

"Hard to say." I guess that's not what you expected to hear. But I do know what short writing isn't.

There are many misconceptions about the art of short writing. And yes, the definitions can be poles apart for different people and situations. For a novelist who writes thousand-page manuscripts, the concept of a novella could, and probably does, seem daunting and vice versa. The short story writer may struggle with a tagline (pitch) or a Tweet. But a great standup comic with a knack for one-liners knows what timing and writing short is all about.

Let's begin with the misconceptions:

1. The first misconception about writing short is that it isn't hard to do. *Really? False! Have you tried it?*
2. The second is that short stories hold no prominence in the literary world. *False! Like short films they may get little respect. Some of the most important stories we experience in our lives are short ones.*
3. Short stories or novellas don't have enough meat to them to tell a good tale or relay a moral. *Again, false. Not when they're done right. Instead, consider how short stories like Grimm's Faerie Tales taught life lessons to children with simple (albeit frightening) examples.*

The key misconception about writing short is discerning it isn't about taking a big story and leaving out a lot of stuff. This interpretation couldn't be more misguided. Why? Because it's not about what's missing, it's about what the author chooses to include.

No one considered the marble Michelangelo removed while creating David. It was all about the marble he chose to keep. So writing short is not about leaving stuff out, it is about the quality and importance about what's left behind. The essential difference between writing short and writing long is actually what the writer chooses to include for the reader.

Writing long means an author can create a bigger story, have more characters, a larger plot, more conflict, more events—bigger, larger, more...more...more.

The most important thing to consider about writing short is to leave the reader satisfied, whether you're writing a tagline, a promo, or a novella.

NOTES

2 Chapter - Condense the Idea

The very first notion you should come to accept when writing short is the idea of condensing the story concept. Then, take the premise you want to write, and carefully construct a hypothesis sentence.

Ugh! I know. You're asking, "Wh-what is a hypothesis sentence, again?"

Merriam Webster says, "It's an assumption, supposition, or concession made for the sake of argument. An idea or theory that is not proven but one that leads to further study or discussion. A premise."

Simply an idea sentence. Call it your idea.

You remember picking a subject you didn't want to write about and having to come up with an "idea" sentence. You probably hated doing hypothesis sentences when you were in high school, whether it was for writing a story, doing a project, or writing a thesis. But to abridge the idea for your purpose, it is now crucial.

Think about what you are planning to write or what you are presently writing. For this book, my title states the obvious hypothesis: *Writing for maximum impact means saying more with less*. Therefore, summarizing the essence is critical in order to satisfy the reader when you have fewer words to work with.

So it's important to condense plot, words, and the number of characters in order to precisely impart your story. It's inconceivable to take a story like *War and Peace* and think to truncate it into a satisfying short story. You can create a concept sentence or theme sentence for a long novel, but what you leave out is the scope of work. To write something short based on a tome such as *War and Peace*, a better possibility would be to take some singular event from the epic, a point or example you want to make, and focus on that detail to write about.

NOTES

3 Chapter - Why Write Short?

We see more examples today than ever before of writing short because of social media. Does anyone spell out a full word anymore? Or speak in complete sentences? When you write for your audience, pick what works for the media.

Therefore, you can be more effective in a short period of time if you can summarize your thoughts and story or purpose.

So why is this important to writers? How does short writing apply to the novelist?

Well, you've heard of the elevator pitch, right? The pitch you can give in an elevator before you reach your floor. If some agent, publisher, or editor turns to you and says, "Gee, what's your story about?" You want to be prepared to reply in one simple, concise sentence; a sentence that grabs attention so you have time to go on and explain your story in a little more detail.

What does it take to get that kind of attention? What will it take to have him asking for more? What if he requests the book? What if he requests a synopsis? How can you write a synopsis short or long enough to fit his criteria? Perhaps once it's completely written you know too much detail about your book to make the choices between what to include and what to leave out.

Even so, it's difficult without the proper tools.

Knowledge.

If a short summary is requested, how can you explain your hundred-thousand word book in one page? Since a synopsis is usually written before your book, and the purpose of it is to help you stay on task, you may have written a long detailed synopsis before you write the book. Once the book is fully written, it's more difficult for you to figure out where to cut the outline down. Perhaps you know too much detail about your book to make effective choices about what to include and what to leave out. Try choosing your favorite child.

That's where the secret of writing short comes in handy. Those ten pages have extraneous words and those ten pages have less important points you've made that you could skip over.

Focus on goal, motivation, and conflict. Focus on your over-arcing plot.

Putting it into as few words as possible, making those few words count. Use words that will entice the reader to read your book.

NOTES

4 CHAPTER – WHAT TO KEEP

Writing requires, or at the very least involves, thinking about what you're going to write before you write it. Pantsers and plotters alike, either vomit up ideas or think them through, step by step, as they are writing. (Wait! Plotters, swiftly prevent your pantser friends from tossing down this book and walking away now! Thank you.)

Pantsers, there's nothing different in your method from what I'm suggesting. You have the natural ability to keep ideas and lists in your heads. So think your plan through using the concepts in this book, and you and your plotter friends will arrive at the same place eventually.

Writing short is nothing more than condensing the story concept to the smallest common plot core. We pick out the essence of an event we choose to write about, and select the most important things about what happens in a restricted period of time. Jot down notes, choose the ideas with the most merit, and discard the rest.

In order to write short, we choose fewer character archetypes, focus on the main characters, and a singular [exciting, not boring] plot. The goal still is to produce a complete, compelling story. The difference is how effectively we use precise action verbs, descriptive nouns, and diverse sentence structure to create action with varied pace. We do the same thing in longer novels with bigger stories, but in short writing we have a tighter focus.

Imagine using a wide lens camera lens and describing the details as a scene plays out before us. Now imagine what we would see if we zoomed in on the same scene with a telephoto lens. Our perspective would naturally change with what we could see from the new point of view. The details would change and so would the story.

Size doesn't make the tale less informative, or interesting, or satisfying, but it can enable the author to concentrate on a smaller plot. So in planning our story, we decide where the camera lens will focus and visualize the plot from inside the eye of the camera.

Now we know what our story is about, how do we decide what to include in our plot and what to discard. Do we wait until our first edits or our first revision? I once heard Dean Koontz describe his writing method and thought it was a useful process for writing either short or long.

He writes his daily chapter or chapters. The following day, he quickly edits what he did the previous day and picks up his writing where he left off. He keeps the flow going. When his book is written, the preliminary edits are already finished. The first round of edits is complete, and the book is ready for revision one. All the tightening and minor corrections were accomplished as he wrote, with his ideas still fresh in his mind. Ready for revision one, he can identify any overstated aspects of the book or add anything he may have missed.

There are ways to adjust any method to any writing style. Writing short isn't about writing style; it's about the size of the story and the word count. What can we say about the subject and how many words do we have to use? Choose your words wisely, always.

NOTES

5 Chapter - The Story Within

Today, stories, movies, and TV programming cater to those with the attention span of a gnat or, more correctly, have spawned and nurtured the elements of a short attention span. Fifteen-second commercials and two minute programming mean you must be able to develop more hooks within your commercial or story to keep the viewer or reader engaged. Would you like to learn what it takes to identify a story within a story? Discover the simple plot? How do you accomplish this?

Go back to the camera lens if all else fails. Identify, find, and include the qualities you enjoy most in anything you read: believable motivation, emotion, pace, vivid details, realistic dialogue, likable/unlikable characters, interesting conflict, attainable goals. Plotters make a list. Pantsers think it through.

How does this apply to fiction writing? Novellas or Novels? What do novels and novellas have in common with fiction writers' needs? Principles of one may apply to the other. Long, involved novels draw readers in, take them to other times, locations, or adventures. Epics make me want to walk inside and close the cover behind me…step through the wide angled lens and experience the adventure. Those novels are the stuff huge best sellers are made of, and I want to read them slowly and leisurely, hold myself back, and never put them down. You know? The ones we hate finishing. I'm a huge fan of books too thick to hold open in my hands.

But every length seems to serve a purpose. The secret of any satisfying read is well developed characters and plot to fit the length. Consider what we write when we have specific/limited word counts for everything we do.

Look at the style of writing we're exposed to daily: Short—Concise—Direct.

On the subject of shorts, there are certain aspects of writing that must be applied. The professional commercial writer has experience. There is the need to create shorts to identify the story, promo blips, tag lines and log lines, long and short synopsis and blurbs. So the professional author has probably already done short writing without even thinking about it. Yet many struggle with some aspects because there's a true art to condensing words, thoughts, characters, and plot ideas effectively.

There are various other purposes for shorts. Newspapers and magazine articles fulfill our needs for short non-fiction information we don't get on the hundred and forty character social media sites, yet there's a dynamic market for short fiction, too. I have friends who actually read newspapers. *"True Romance"*, *"True Confessions"*, and other magazines are still around and selling even though they aren't as convenient as choosing what we want when we want it on our electronic reader.

With the advent of the e-reader we have the ability to read news, short stories, and short fiction in almost any genre we want, in any location, in novella or novel format, on our e-readers or phones. I don't have to read the AARP article in the doctor's office. I can read a cute sci-fi romance in space or a sexy Valentine surprise while I'm waiting for the dentist. Both do a better job of taking my mind off where I am better than the material in their office that's already making my mouth ache.

We can escape into fiction wherever we go. Fight a dragon, win a princess, climb a mountain, storm a castle.

The advantage of a short, satisfying lunch-time read is the way we can reach that happily ever after and put a smile on our face before we head back to work. Read a good story and change our attitude. Have you noticed how short *"The Chicken Soup for the Soul"* stories are? *"Reader's Digest"* was popular and still is for a good reason. Example-driven advice has more impact when it's short and delivered concisely. The stories are interesting, quick paced, and provide the reader with a message.

Poof! We're done, and when we look up from the story with a new attitude or insight, we can go back to the real world with a different perspective. The same can be said for any good short fiction.

NOTES

6 CHAPTER - WORDS THAT COUNT

Writing a novella? Word choice equals impact. We don't have the luxury of more words like Tolkien or Michener. Our quest is to achieve more with less.

Word Choices in Short Books:

Make correct word choices—the most effective verb, the most unique noun, or a descriptive sense to create the spirit of the moment. Don't fool around. Tighten the prose until it squeals.

Get right to the point and keep the scene interesting and intriguing without making the story feel rushed.

Use action in every sentence, not necessarily car chases or explosions, but make use of action verbs instead of passive ones.

Clutter prevents the story from moving forward. Clean house and keep a fast pace.

Eliminate or limit extraneous adverbs and adjectives.

What should you cut when there's nothing else? I have a few general suggestions...

Let's try some exercises:

1. Check your (adjectives) descriptives. If you can use one instead of two or three, pick one effective word that fits best.
2. This is true for adverbs as well.
3. Choose more descriptive verbs in your sentences. "Glared" instead of "looked menacingly" becomes more active writing.
4. Cut the superfluous (anything that isn't vital) to move the story or scene forward. Too much or unnecessary narrative, and description. Restating the obvious, wallowing in too much deep point of view, wordy dialogue, and unnecessary dialogue tags.
5. Rewrite sentences from past perfect tense. Make them active and engaging. Removes passive language and busy words.

NOTES

7 CHAPTER - TAGLINES, BLURBS, SYNOPSIS

We write short because, in this day and age, with so much coming at us, it's very difficult to absorb everything we are exposed to. Social media, electronics, and information bombard us at hyper-speed. Media fights for a parking spot in our brains and often, out of necessity, it double parks.

We encounter, perhaps, an equal number of commercial breaks on commercial TV during the course of one program as we do the actual story we are trying to appreciate. And watching the news and weather…that's almost frightening.

During the news, tickertape is running underneath, and not always just one. Additional boxes are in the lower left-hand corner, one in the upper left-hand corner, and another in the background behind the newscaster. To decipher a weather forecast, we have to interpret radar maps overlaid on road maps and multiple inputs on the screen at the same time, merely to get a hint of the temperature or the forecast of rain in the morning.

It's difficult to sort through the screen shots and pay attention to the massive amount of information. We are constantly making choices about what we want to watch, hear, or read.

Readers become comfortable with what they read most often. These days, the reader is bombarded with social media and media distributed by electronic means. We have become familiar with the use of pictures, images, and symbols used to replace the written word. Visual impressions are singularly more effective than words.

Twitter has become the home of hashtags and anagrams, and emoji's have taken over Face Book. I'm "happy dancing" or "smiling" or "thumbs up liking" something all day, every day. I no longer need to fully express what I think. I can skirt the details and use an emoji shortcut to "high-five" my friend on her graduation or "heart" her on her birthday. OMG…we can't write short enough to satisfy the new short cuts.

Think of taglines as one-liners we can post in a Tweet, and loglines as movie or TV short descriptions. Not exactly the same thing, but close. TV/movie descriptions are loglines, usually good examples so we know what the TV program is going to be about but in a condensed version. After flipping through the cable guide, we can apply our book ideas in a similar way. Because of electronic books, the back cover blurb or inside cover flap have been replaced with long and short blurbs, cover taglines or author quotes, and the need for different sizes is necessary to get the reader's attention on websites and buy sites. So getting those tools right becomes imperative to selling books.

Blurbs: The Essence of Plot. All fiction writing should emphasize the following, especially blurbs...

Who are the main characters?
What do they want? (G)
Why do they want it? (M)
What prevents them from achieving this goal? (C)
What consequences will they face if they don't reach the goal? (M)

Who wants what? His or her goal.
What prevents them from attaining what they want individually/together? The conflict.
What consequences will they face if they don't accomplish their goal/s? This is motivation.

In romance we include both the hero and heroine unless the book is written in first person or a single point of view. All other times, the point of view character is our focus character.

Who is she? What does she want? What is keeping her from getting it? What will be the result of failing?

The second paragraph should cover the same questions regarding the hero.

A third paragraph is the summation of the potential consequence of failure or the success of achieving the goal. We often see it posed as a question, which is becoming cliché.

In summation for romance writing, the blurb needs to address the following basic four precepts for each character to deliver maximum effect.

Consider how we write a synopsis.

The synopsis is the skeleton of our book. The length, long or short, depends on how much detail about the story the author chooses to include on the framework. By adding organs, nerves, blood vessels, muscles, skin, and hair, an entire body is built on the bones the way an author builds a story with details on a synopsis. How much of the details—characters, action, events, locations, goals, conflicts, motivations, and resolutions—that the author includes in the synopsis determines the length.

If you've ever tried to submit your book for contests or publication, everyone seems to want a different size synopsis. Pantsers may want to disregard this advice because it's not part of their process, but I also have a suggestion to help you with writing the synopsis after the fact.

Usually before I write the book, I have a good outline of what I think I'm going to have in the story...mentally, if not on paper. Then I like to bullet point my ideas before I write a long synopsis, which includes a lot of detail. I believe it's easier for me to shorten my synopsis than lengthen it. I highlight the key points until I have three different size synopses, which I can use for several purposes. I can easily shrink the longer one if I have an agent or an editor who wants to see a shorter version. Sometimes the original can be anywhere from one page to ten pages, or more. And I like to whittle it down to blurb points. I can then create long and short blurbs and loglines this way.

Now you can also do the same with the book. Write a long version, but then when you realize the call for submission requires a shorter version, don't panic about slicing and dicing. When the time comes, some books can't be cut without removing the heart of the plot. The concept is too large. If the book contains subplots that weave through the main plot you may be able to cut a subplot or two if they aren't intrinsic to the main plot resolution. I prefer going from short to long rather than going long to short, because some things just can't be cut without making the book feel chopped.

Cutting a long version may seem as if there was poor planning up front, or the plot wasn't well developed...or that the story is going in circles.

Make a list of important points about your story characters and plot points before you begin. Add everything you want to the list, and then go back and strike out all the elements that won't work or aren't necessary in a short version, either because they aren't essential to hooking a reader and moving the main plot forward, or because they complicate the plot and make writing it short or condensing it impossible. What is outside the scope of vision in your plan?

Sweep away the dust and use what's left to sculpt your masterpiece.

NOTES

8 CHAPTER – CHARACTERS: FEWER ARCHETYPES.

Use a limited number of characters to tell the story, especially in blurbs. This doesn't mean we're going to short sheet the reader. So how?

Combine prototypes whenever possible: The sidekick with the mentor. The heroine with the caregiver. The antagonist with the hero.

The complete lists of archetypes vary by name and characteristics. The Innocent - The Orphan/Regular Guy or Gal - The Hero - The Caregiver - The Explorer - The Lover - The Rebel - The Jester - The Creator - The Sage - The Magician - The Ruler

How do other elements affect these characters? They may have multiple characteristics. Are archetypes always all black or white? Not usually. Or do we find elements of other types within our characters? More often than not.

Based on Carl G. Jung's theory of the myth, the classics are symbolic elements containing aspects of the workings of human life and mind. What archetypes are absolutely necessary in a suspense story? An antagonist of sorts. Certainly the Explorer (perhaps the detective). What about a romantic suspense? We need the Lovers and the Magician or Ruler, perhaps the Rebel.

Using *Star Wars* as an example, George Lucas made use of many of Joseph Campbell's archetypes from *The Hero With A Thousand Faces*, in his epics, but in stories like *Of Mice and Men* by John Steinbeck many of the characteristics of the traditional classics archetypes were combined into singular characters. Often in romances, the hero or heroine can play the antagonist and protagonist, depending on the point of view character's perspective.

Why does it matter? The Sage might also be the Ruler and the Hero. The smaller you write the more important it is to combine these characteristics. You don't need to include all the archetypes in every story, but depending on the plot, you may need a few of their characteristics to carry out the story line. Try analyzing a few movies or TV shows looking at these character types.

NOTES

9 CHAPTER - SHORT IS ABOUT PACING

What is writing short all about? Pacing. If all the words and sounds on the page read the same or feel too similar the reading gets boring. The emphasis is the same for every word and sentence. The sentence structure is the same throughout.

Flat, boring, dull. I'm ready to snooze. The monotone puts us to sleep or we can't stay focused on the subject.

ZZZZ BAM! Wake up! Shorten sentences. Words. Place emphasis where the reader won't expect it. Use different words and sentence arrangement to change the reader's mood. Change the pace.

When we write short, creating good pacing is important. We have a minimal number of words to create that special mood. Don't waste any words making it happen.

What about Sentence Structure? How we structure our sentences increases or decreases the emphasis on the words we choose. Vary your sentence structure and make it interesting. If the house burns down before the reader finishes our story, what do we want the reader to take away or remember from the experience? What will make the reader want to continue where he/she left off...before dinner needed to be prepared, or the phone rang, or the world flipped upside down?

To keep the reader engrossed, authors can effectively use hooks where emphasis ends on the short sentence. The hook, based on balanced sentence structure and placement is even more important than wording in short writing than in longer, traditionally written novels, papers, or articles. Short isn't simple. Short is word magic.

NOTES

10 Chapter – Dialogue as a Tool

How does dialogue affect length? Authors can use dialogue effectively to write shorter works. Tags can be replaced with short, descriptive narrative showing something important about the character, action, location, or scene. Even then, it should express the necessary information with impact. Too much or wordy narrative slows the pace. I recommend *Pitfalls to avoid: Dialogue by John Hewitt/About Writing* if you have questions about writing dialogue.

When writing shorter stories, using dialogue correctly can be a powerful tool. But if used incorrectly it can destroy pacing. The author must delete stilted, unnatural speech (identify and remove filler) and eliminate dialogue that doesn't further the scene or develop the characters. Well-written dialogue picks up the pace and advances the story line.

We must remove exposition dialogue (that stuff when the character explains the plot, or backstory to a friend, and repeats information for the benefit of the reader). Writing dialogue poorly can have as negative an effect on pace as writing too much narrative can. Instead of being useful, modifiers often become annoying. Readers are capable of assuming the obvious if the author has done a good job of showing the story. Do not bury the reader in unnecessary detail, and please do not directly name characters, or over use dialogue modifiers.

Remove redundancy and repetition, anywhere and everywhere. Eliminate every paragraph, every sentence, and every word that does not move the story forward. If it's boring or mundane or overstated get rid of it.

The purpose of dialogue can be one of the following: it should advance plot or show power shift between characters, create immediacy, reveal character, create emotional impact, begin or heighten conflict, or create suspense…and always…dialogue should accelerate the pace.

NOTES

11 CHAPTER – PACE CREATES MOOD

Things that affect pace…and as a result, affect mood. Word choices. Varied word choices give the structure impact and rhythm. Every word and every sentence should have a reason for being, but not every word carries as much emphasis or weight as another. Sentence structure also affects mood and pace, and not every sentence should have the same clout as every other. Never forget to show the scene, don't tell it. Whether it's in narrative or dialogue, only show the reader what is necessary. Showing the story unfold, rather than telling the story, puts the reader in the action.

Inconsequential details slow pace, confuse the reader, take away from the important information, and as a result sets the readers up to begin skimming. The readers' eyes glaze over until an interesting word or phrase jumps off the page and grabs them back into the story. How far will the readers skim before the doorbell rings and they put the story down for good?

Beware! If it happens too often, the reader may not return. And since we're talking about writing short, we don't have the word count to waste to allow for skimming.

Here are a few effective tips to keep the reader interested:
1. Use short paragraphs.
2. Include white space.
3. Apply sharp, crisp verbs and sentences with punch.
4. Think about advertising techniques.
5. Think in fragments.

All this affects pace and pace creates mood. How do we do this when we're writing short? To review, word choice is key. Being capable of describing our work in progress in one sentence will help, too. Choose every word carefully to express the key elements in every scene. What is the mood?

Is the story a love story?

Happy, sad, or tragic?

Are the relationships easy, loving ones or a highly conflicted ones with hidden secrets?

Is it an action story with danger greeting the characters at every turn?

Go ahead. See what you come up with... Now expand your concept into two sentences. Use the same criteria. Make the words count. How about trying three sentences next?

Now evaluate your sentences. What's the mood/tone/pace? Did you choose descriptive words that fit?

NOTES

12 CHAPTER – HOOK THE READER

Short writing must hook the reader immediately. When we write short we don't have time for the beautiful flowing narrative. Adjectives and adverbs become extraneous if not precise. Word choice is essential. Consider the words and choose carefully, pick exactly. If we are writing a long blurb about our book, for instance, we wisely consider the two hundred and fifty words limit.

We can afford to use a number of words that describe what's going on in our story. But when our blurb/tag is twenty-five words, we are going to have to go back to those two hundred and fifty words and extract the ones with the most impact.

Emotional body-language description increases the size of our narrative. Choose precise, descriptive, emotion words or action words to condense narrative.

A few examples:
1. grief - contort, collapse, sob, tremble
2. happiness - dance, swirl, giggle, delight
3. anger - frown, clench

In "*How to Write Short: Word Craft for Fast Times*" Roy Peter Clark (The Poynter Institute) Little, Brown and Company; Reprint edition (August 19, 2014) states sentence structure should be precise for impact. I highly recommend reading his book for entertainment and educational purposes. He points out how the use of contrast creates surprise.

The effect, like the idea and title for one of the most successful movie/TV projects in the 90's, is a good example. *Buffy, Teen Vampire Slayer* creates impact. Contemplate how the contrast of her name and the fact she's a teen vampire slayer create the surprising concept. She's a lovely, popular teenaged girl who discovers not only are there demons in her world, but she is destined to become a vampire slayer. The conflict is compounded by the vampire she's attracted to who struggles with his craving to take Buffy's blood, as well as his desire to take her.

The program is filled with symbolism and metaphors for many complex emotional and social issues of the day. With all the paranormal books and movies out since, Buffy may not sound nearly as unique as it was at the time, but creator, Josh Whedon continues to construct new boundaries.

Another short contrasting title example is one I used before. *War and Peace*. Is there any better example of contrast than those two words? Is there surprise in using those words joined with a conjunction such as "and"?

Word choice and placement influences so much about us writers, what we write, and how and what we say with those words.

It's not always what we say, or how we say it, but it's also where we place the emphasis. The word we start the sentence with and the one we end with determines emphasis.

Structure should be intentional to enhance the full impact. And in short writing…greeting cards to ad logos…we experience the maximum impact from the shortest sentences and ideas, and with the "full stop period".

Right? Right.

Clark encourages the use of the period for a full stop, saying it is highly effective for emphasis. Think about it.

Who knew?

We did.

But do we consciously think about it? Consider it? Practice or appreciate it? Do we use the full stop period (or question mark) for what it can create by hooking the reader or in our sentences to create pacing?

The *full stop period* becomes another tool in our toolbox for effectively writing short. Reduce the long, drawn out description, comma delineated parenthetical clauses and extraneous modifiers, and write an effective fragment.

"Just do it." [*Grin.*] Nike 1988

Think of a few other effective short statements to slam the reader with maximum impact.

"I love you."

"Marry me."

"You're fired." (Or, hired.)

"Get out."

"Amen."

Can you think of a few other all-time standard rhetoric from movies or TV that became classics?

One romantic one I recall from the movie, *Jerry Macguire* is "You complete me." From *A Few Good Men* there was "You can't handle the truth." *Field of Dreams* contains another good example, though often misquoted, "If you build it he will come." And, "People will come, Ray."

"Eat Mor Chikin!" Chick-fil-A 1995.

"Eat Fresh" Subway 2000.

"Do the Dew" Mountain Dew 1996.

"Coke is it!" Coca-Cola 1982.

"Got Milk?" California Milk Processor Board 1993.

"It's finger lickin' good." KFC.

There are many more examples, some quite long, but the ones I remember most are the shortest. And if we think of logos, Nike's swish or Apple's bitten apple, the logo can be even more effective than the word ad, but only once we experience the product. The image is only as good as the way it makes you feel about the product because there are no words to tell you.

A picture of a beer bottle dripping with condensation shows us the beer is cold, implies it will be thirst quenching, but add a person who's perspiring, holding the beer with a smile, and it says even more. Add a crowd in the back-ground by a pool and it's a party.

Words work the same way. Add what we need to get our idea across, but keep it simple.

Clark also points out the usefulness and importance of hooks and white space. The well-known observation prevents the words from intimidating the reader and draws attention to the hook. In movies or commercials we can "feel" the white space in the pauses in action or dialogue.

Writers can hook the reader by adding the *shortest* sentence to the end of the paragraph. The tension of a short sentence creates suspension and temporary resolution. But the reader wants more…the hook.

More ideas on sentence structure from author, Roy Peter Clark include breaking down sentences to find the *focal* point. He suggests constructing the order of words by making a decision about which will be the most effective way of writing the beginning, the middle, or the end. Which part will have the greatest impact?*

[*"How to Write Short: Word Craft for Fast Times" by Roy Peter Clark (The Poynter Institute) Little, Brown and Company; Reprint edition (August 19, 2014).]

NOTES

13 CHAPTER - Plotting Scene Elements

Plotting scene elements helps the writer organize the action. Consider the plot for any story. In most cases, we'll be telling the hero's journey. In an interesting story, every scene in the character's story contains goal, motivation, and conflict. These elements move the story forward. What do we include in the shortest writing? The same elements we would in a big story, only fewer of them. Never forget, the short story is just that...short (small)...in contrast to the big story which, therefore, must be naturally long to include the necessary details for a satisfying experience.

Sandra Scofield[1], an award winning American novelist, essayist, editor and author of writers' guides, claims there are four basic scene elements: Event and Emotion, Purpose, Structure, and Pulse.

I interpret Scofield's premise this way:

Purpose as Goal. Structure as Motivation. And Pulse as Conflict.

Then according to Debra Dixon[2] external GMC pushes the action while internal GMC creates the emotional mood. These elements should be in everything we write. And in order to have a satisfying story, at some point, the character must learn something.

This is as good a place as any to include information about goal, motivation, and conflict using the simplest forms: The tagline and blurb. We can use the structure of a blurb as an example to demonstrate GMC in a very simple format.

Open the blurb with an event or emotion as we are introduced to the character's goal or purpose.

We discover the character's motivation in the structure of his world and find out the conflict preventing the event from happening, thus the pulse or energy of the story. The final line is the conclusion or could be an effective tagline.

The tagline should equal the life lesson: or, what did the character learn?

Debra Dixon is the author of ten books, contributor to twelve anthologies, former Vice-President of Romance Writers of America, developer of novel writing courses, also wrote GMC: Goal, Motivation, and Conflict now in its ninth printing from her popular workshop by the same name, she's also President of BelleBooks and its imprint Bell Bridge Books.

[1 *Information from The Scene Book: A Primer for The Fiction Writer by Sandra Scofield.*]

[[2]Dixon, Debra. *Goal, Motivation and Conflict: The Building Blocks of Good Fiction.* Gryphon Books for Writers, 1999.]

NOTES

14 CHAPTER - DEMYSTIFY THE PARTS

Break down the story plot into sections. Screenwriting structure sometimes helps a writer simplify the mystery of organizing the plot. Let's use an example from a screen-play for a one hundred-minute movie.

The standard for screenwriting is one written page equals one movie minute. If you've never studied a script, you should take a look at one. Dialogue, action, and narrative are quite different from most books. If anything has changed in novel writing in recent years, I'd say it is the resemblance to script writing. There's more dialogue. It's snappy, punchy, and to the point—not the long monologues from bygone days. And bare bones narrative appears to be present only to give the reader what's absolutely necessary. In scripts, the narrative is usually reserved for a brief description of the location, the director's instructions to the actor, or the description of the action.

In novels, when deep point of view can't be shown in dialogue or action, narrative is used, but minimally. For instance, an actor can show so much more complicated emotion with actions, facial expression, or voice inflection than an author can state simply by writing the narrative into the scene.

A picture truly is worth a thousand words. I repeat, word choices matter more when condensing the concept.

As a result, the visual action, even if someone just scratches his or her head, increases the pace. The action, a sign of confusion, quickly shows the reader this without going deep into the character's thoughts and feelings. The momentum of the story streams forward.

Today everything is based on a quick pace. Gone are the days when readers leisurely became lost in the word choices of an author, or appreciated and analyzed the flow of the prose. Get on with the story?

What's the point? What happens next? Using script writing as a template for a story set up, we can interject pages for minutes and vice versa. When analyzing some of the best movies, the setup takes place in the first ten percent (or on average, ten minutes for a hundred minute film) therefore ten pages. Using the standard word count per page, we can do the math based on what we plan to write. I don't want your eyes glazing over so we aren't going to take out our calculators. But a good estimate of a very basic line graph shows you how it works.

This is an interpretation of a paradigm of Syd Field's "Three Act Structure," one of my favorites, because of the simplicity, for demonstrating story structure in the form of screenwriting. According to screen writer, Syd Field, in the first one to ten minutes of the film, right up to the inciting incident/first pinch point (where something is going to change), we will:

Meet the main characters, discovers their goals, motivations, and conflicts. Next the viewer observes the over-arching plot when it is revealed and the setting or location will be obvious (especially if it's important to the plot).

As a consequence, the viewers decide the following: Are we interested in the plot? Do we care about what happens to the characters? Is the concept interesting, and is the pace enough to keep us watching? If we decide to continue watching, the story unfolds during the final ninety percent:

➢ from the first plot point (something changes)
➢ to the rising action (conflicts)
➢ to the mid peak (point of no return)
➢ tumbling to the black moment (all hope is lost)
➢ then the climax (success or failure)
➢ finally the conclusion (transformation)

What happens and how the viewer perceives the film during this period depends on pacing and balance. It is the same in writing, no matter the length of the book. We've all seen variations on this timeline but I use this for simple form from everything from plot structure to taglines.

Whether it's ten thousand words or one hundred-thousand words, we can divide up our story into the same template for success. The first ten percent comprises the ordinary world until something changes, and then we follow that with the inciting incident and rising conflict.

At the fifty percent mark things should begin to fall apart right up to the black moment at the ninety percent point when it looks like all is doomed to failure. You have ten percent left to reach the climax and wrap things up. Everything must be resolved.

*Field, Syd. Screenplay: The Foundations of Screenwriting. Dell Publishing Company, Inc. 1984.

*Vogler, Christopher. The Writer's Journey: Mythic Structure for Writers. Michael Wiese Productions, 1998.

*Campbell, Joseph. The Hero with a Thousand Faces. 1st edition, Bollingen Foundation, 1949. 2nd edition, Princeton University Press. 3rd edition, New World Library, 2008.

NOTES

15 CHAPTER - WHAT'S YOUR BOOK ABOUT?

Since each scene and chapter should contain goal, motivation, and conflict, the author can write a story with a quick satisfying pace while providing a plot with clarity. The reader has enough information to understand the plot immediately and be committed to the characters. Curiosity drives the reader from one hook (to find out what happens next) to the next.

But what is your book about? Based on the need for goal, motivation, and conflict in even the smallest dimension of our writing, we should be able to write anything from a Tagline (Tweet) to an epic saga using the same formula. The template also applies to series books, because we should use the same format when we begin writing the over-arching plot line for a series, then again for each individual segment of the series.

Let's view loglines and examine a few examples from some TV series. Which ones could use more descriptive words to draw interest?

The Twilight Zone (1959) Creator Rod Serling This groundbreaking anthology series presents tales of the supernatural often with social commentary.

Lost (1994) After their plane crashes on a deserted island a diverse group of people must adapt to their new home and its enigmatic forces.

White Collar (2009) To avoid jail a super suave ex-con man joins forces with his FBI handler to catch other white-collar thieves while concealing his ulterior motive.

Criminal Minds (2005) An intense police procedural series follows a group of FBI profilers as they get into the minds of psychopathic killers.

Friends (1994) This merry sitcom follows the daily misadventures of six twenty something pals as they navigate the pitfalls of love, life, and work in Manhattan.

The similarity between loglines and pitches is remarkable. Being able to condense our book down to the primary concept will give us an advantage when we are asked that daunting question, "So…what's your book about?"

"Choke. Gasp. Sputter."

J.K. Rowling could have said, "My book, *Harry Potter*, is about a young boy, rescued from neglect, who faces his destiny to be a great wizard."

Some other generic examples:

1. "The heroine falls in love with a fireman but is conflicted by fear because she was orphaned after losing her family in a house fire."
2. "A spaceship from Earth lands on Mars to begin colonization only to discover other beings have already laid their claim."

Simply put, the main character wants something (goal) for some reason (motivation) and something is keeping him/her from getting it (conflict).

Now make it sound interesting and expand each part a little more.

1. After three months of dating Josh, Katie is ready to let down her guard and admit he is the one, at least until the fire sirens go off in the small town where he lives. Four years earlier, she'd lost everything to a house fire, including her family. When she discovers Josh is a volunteer fireman she isn't prepared to face her fear of losing another loved one to the flames, but he's determined to convince her he's going nowhere, and loving her is the only chance he's taking.

2. All the research said an outpost habitation on Mars was possible, but Commander Allan Pit wasn't prepared for what he and the colonists found inside the caves. With nowhere to go, they were prepared to fight for the right to stay, but so were the aliens who'd lost their home planet and colonized earlier. They were more suited to the rugged environment, and without fuel, returning to Earth wasn't a viable option for Allan's crew unless the secret about Mars proved true.

Those could be longer or shorter. For the romance enthusiasts, we can combine the hero's and heroine's goals, motivations, and conflicts in the blurb for the romance as well as the secondary plot line if there is one. The romance below is also a suspense so there are two plot lines; one for the romance and one for the suspense.

Here are three examples of a summation and taglines from the romantic suspense novella by Eliza March, *Trouble in the Tropics*.

Summation: Cyber terrorists try to prevent a doctorate student on spring break from completing her thesis when they discover her project could undermine their recent plans to hack into military files.

Here are two taglines, but we could write more depending upon what we choose to emphasize:

TAG 1: Before doctorate student Sage Demings graduates and is shuffled off to the NSA, she vows to experience one spring break even if it kills her.

TAG 2: Cyber security specialist Ryan O'Malley takes a busman's holiday when the sexy coed he's partying with turns out to be his assignment.

Each gives the reader a different perspective on the story. One may appeal to one reader and one to another. Next let's examine how to handle the short blurb.

SHORT: *Cyber specialist, Sage Deming committed herself to the NSA after spring break, her first—hot sun, white sand, and mindless sex—until a series of deadly encounters threaten to interrupt her plans.*

Colonel Ryan O'Malley returns after a two-year deployment with a goal to relax before his next cyber security assignment. Is it just dumb luck or fate he's there when the co-ed he's interested in is almost run down?

Now the LONGER version.

LONG: *PhD student, Sage Deming committed herself to the NSA, but not until after taking her first spring break—hot sun, white sand, and mindless sex. But then a series of deadly encounters threaten to interrupt her plans.*

Colonel Ryan O'Malley returns after a two-year deployment with a goal to relax before his next cyber security assignment. Is it just dumb luck he's there when the first hot chick he encounters is almost run down and kidnapped?

Facing danger and betrayal, Sage and Ryan discover a cyber terrorist plot to keep her from finishing her project for Homeland Security.

That she's determined to experience all spring break has to offer, including casual sex, strangely rankles Ryan as much as the possibility she's a terrorist target. He's determined to protect her and fulfill her qualifications for that weekend fling.

Sage discovers there's more to life than work, and more to love than she's experienced, but will she manage to stay alive long enough to enjoy it? If the government and her handsome colonel have any say, she will not only finish her project, she'll get more than the spring break she's been waiting for.

In fact, we can go longer or shorter as the whim or need dictates.

Whatever we are comfortable doing drives the direction we take. We can use the large idea and break it down, or take the core and expand it. Discover our intent and define it. If one way stumps us, we can try another, as long as we always return to the heart of the story to find our primary plot and our characters' GMC. The core of our story wiill always be the rock we build on or chip away at.

NOTES

16 CHAPTER - Secrets of Writing Short

Secrets of writing short: Understanding the art of writing short will come in handy the way algebra helps you in everyday life. As soon as you need it this will all make sense. Frankly it can't hurt to apply many of these same techniques to writing "long" either. In summation, review the following and see if you can break down your WIP by using a few of these techniques. It never hurts to tighten your writing.

Simplify Plot - Focus on the major goal, motivation, and conflict for your book, and determine the over-arching plot of what you choose to describe. Goals, realistically driven by motivation, based on inner conflict, and complicated by external conflict are the most engaging. Remove anything that hints of a subplot when writing a short story or novella.

Combine Archetypes - Stick to main characters in blurbs or tags. Eliminate all extraneous characters and combine character archetypes into as few as possible in short works.

Careful Word Choice - Put the ideas into as few words as possible, and make those few words count. Use words that will entice readers and keep them reading. Precise word choice for action and description creates more with less.

Effective Narrative – Sentence structure, placement, and choice effects mood and pace. Even word sounds and rhythm can have an impact on the mood and pace of the story.

Necessary Dialogue – What the characters say, and how or when they say it is an interesting way of giving the reader information about the character or situation without dragging in backstory or deep point of view—another way to say more with less.

Jerry (Tom Cruise) opens his heart to Dorothy (Renée Zellweger) in an example of iconic catch phrases. The following phrase now a symbol of expressed affection, was popularized by the movie Jerry Maguire*. At the end of the movie, when Jerry expresses his love in a long-winded speech to Dorothy, her simple reply was, "…You had me at 'hello'."

"Hook 'em fast, keep 'em reading, and leave 'em satisfied."©

[*1996 American romantic comedy-drama sports film written, produced and directed by Cameron Crowe.]

NOTES

17 CHAPTER – REFERENCES AND RECOMMENDATIONS

Ballenger, Bruce and Barry Lane. Discovering the Writer Within: 40 Days to More Imaginative Writing. Writer's Digest Books, 1989.

Bickham, Jack. Scene and Structure. Writer's Digest Books, 1999.

Campbell, Joseph. The Hero with a Thousand Faces. 1st edition, Bollingen Foundation, 1949. 2nd edition, Princeton University Press. 3rd edition, New World Library, 2008.

Clark, Roy Peter. How to Write Short: Word Craft for Fast Times. Little, Brown and Company, 2013 edition.

Dixon, Debra. Goal, Motivation and Conflict: The Building Blocks of Good Fiction. Gryphon Books for Writers, 1999.

Field, Syd. Screenplay: The Foundations of Screenwriting. Dell Publishing Company, Inc. 1984.

Frey, James. How to Write a Damn Good Novel: A Step-by-Step No Nonsense Guide to Dramatic Storytelling. St. Martin's Press, 1987.

Gardner, John. The Art of Fiction: Notes of Craft for Young Writers. Vintage, 1991.

King, Stephen. Secret Windows: Essays and Fiction on the Craft of Writing. Book of the Month Club, 2000.

McKee, Robert. Story: Substance, Structure, Style and the Principles of Screenwriting. Regan Books, 1997.

Swain, Dwight. Techniques of the Selling Writer. University of Oklahoma Press, 1982.

Vogler, Christopher. The Writer's Journey: Mythic Structure for Writers. Michael Wiese Productions, 1998.

ABOUT THE AUTHOR

The author may have been born in Manhattan, but she spent the first twenty-one years of her life traveling the world as a military dependent. After her father retired in the Hamptons, she met and married her husband but they couldn't imagine raising a family in the cold weather. Florida sun beckoned! She claims they looked like the Beverly Hillbillies hauling their worldly belongings to the unknown, but five children, three grandchildren, a successful business career, and several animals later, she and her husband are thinking about moving further south.

One thing most people don't know about the author is she once wrote a syndicated gossip column many years before she ever imagined becoming an author or editor. Her first love is reading fiction, her second is writing, and the third is helping other writers attain their goals.

She writes both fiction (as Eliza March) and non-fiction (as Maureen Frances Sevilla), professionally edits, and has been fortunate to work on projects with a few NY Times, USA Today, and Amazon best-selling authors.

Author's Note:

I hope my suggestions help. Frankly, I know it will help me. I'm going make a vow and plaster these lessons on my desk top, and practice what I preach using these ideas as reference material while I write my future work.

It's not always easy to remember to do the preliminary work whether it's on paper or in your head, but I find it sure speeds up the process. One of my best-selling authors is remarkable at doing this. Her books always go out shorter than they come in. But during edits, I notice eliminating the extraneous and picking the "right" word is what she does well.

Thank you for buying this book and please consider leaving a review and a recommendation if you find anything here helpful.

WEB PAGE: http://www.MaureenSevilla.com

EMAIL: Maureen.Sevilla@gmail.com